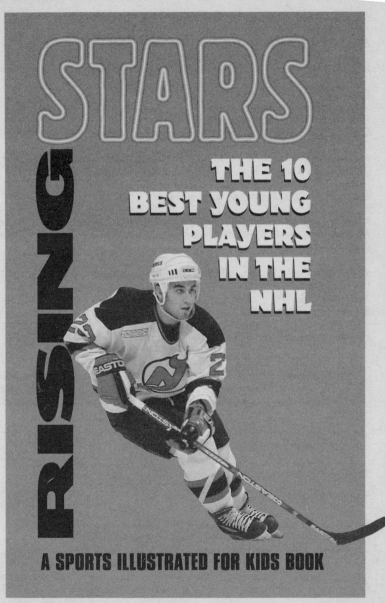

STARS

RISING

THE 10 BEST YOUNG PLAYERS IN THE NHL

A SPORTS ILLUSTRATED FOR KIDS BOOK

Rising Stars: The 10 Best Young Players in the NHL, by Mike Brehm and
Michael Russo
A SPORTS ILLUSTRATED FOR KIDS publication/September 2000

SPORTS ILLUSTRATED FOR KIDS and **KiDS** are registered trademarks of Time Inc.

Front-cover design by Emily Peterson Perez
Interior design by Sherry Summerlin
Research by Steve Pittman and Kathleen Fieffe
Cover photographs: Mitchell Layton/NHL Images (Scott Gomez), John Cordes/Icon SMI
(Paul Kariya), Bob Rosato/Sports Illustrated (Chris Pronger)
Additional photographs: Sports Illustrated: 6, 34, 52, 88 (Lou Capozzola); 16 (Tim
DeFrisco); 25 (David E. Klutho); 42 (Bill Wippert); 61 (Robert Beck); 70, 79
(Darren Carroll)

Rising Stars: The 10 Best Young Players in the NHL is published by SPORTS ILLUSTRATED
FOR KIDS, a division of Time Inc. Its trademark is registered in the U.S. Patent and
Trademark Office and in other countries. SPORTS ILLUSTRATED FOR KIDS, 135 West 50th
St., 4th Floor, New York, N.Y. 10020-1393

For information, address: SPORTS ILLUSTRATED FOR KIDS

ISBN 1-930623-11-9

Printed in the United States of America

10 9 8 7 6 5 4 3 2 1

Rising Stars: The 10 Best Young Players in the NHL is a
production of SPORTS ILLUSTRATED FOR KIDS Books:
Cathrine Wolf, Assistant Managing Editor; Emily Peterson Perez, Art Director;
Margaret Sieck, Senior Editor; Aaron Derr and Jon Kramer (Project Editor),
Associate Editors; Robert J. Rohr, Copy Manager; Erin Tricarico, Photo Researcher;
Ron Beuzenburg, Production Manager

CONTENTS

To my wife, Elizabeth Hurley, and our three
children, Hannah, Matthew, and Rebecca
— *Mike Brehm*

For my family and friends, who have
inspired and encouraged me
— *Michael Russo*

INTRODUCTION

Most hockey fans are familiar with the exploits of such superstars as Jaromir Jagr, Pavel Bure, Dominik Hasek, Steve Yzerman, and Peter Forsberg. But in recent years, some new names have appeared on the scene. Hailing from all corners of the globe, players such as Paul Kariya, Chris Pronger, Scott Gomez, and Milan Hejduk have generated lots of excitement.

You'll meet 10 of this new generation's greatest players in *Rising Stars*.

Rising Stars features plenty of interesting stories. You'll learn how little winger Paul Kariya of the Mighty Ducks of Anaheim excels in a game dominated by giants. You'll read how center Chris Drury of the Colorado Avalanche once pitched his team to a Little League World Series title. You'll find out why defenseman Chris Pronger of the St. Louis Blues was booed so harshly after arriving in St. Louis. And you'll read about winger Jeff Friesen of the San Jose Sharks, who was once picked on by his own teammates.

So turn the page and start reading about these 10 great athletes. Learn about some of the obstacles they faced on the way to the top. And find out why they will be making headlines in the world of hockey for years to come.

Paul has been terrorizing NHL goaltenders since he entered the league in 1994-95.

PAUL KARIYA

Paul takes pride in his ability to out-think the opposition

★★★★★★★★★★★

It's no secret that brothers tend to compete against each other.

Left wing Paul Kariya of the Mighty Ducks of Anaheim and his younger brother, Steve, a left wing for the Vancouver Canucks, have done it a lot since they were kids — and not just in hockey.

"We made everything basically a competition," says Paul, "especially in the summer when we were training, when we were shooting pucks or playing passing games. We'd invent games, and we also loved to play Ping-Pong and everything. I mean, everything that we do — cards, cribbage, checkers."

Great hockey players are extremely competitive. Steve Yzerman, Pavel Bure, Mark Messier — take your pick. Paul is no exception.

"He definitely doesn't like to lose," Steve says.

RISING

Hard Work Pays Off
★★★★★★★★★★★

Paul Tetsuhiko Kariya was born on October 16, 1974, in Vancouver, British Columbia, Canada. He's the second-oldest of five children. His father, Tetsuhiko, is Japanese, and his mother, Sharon, is Canadian. Mr. and Mrs. Kariya were both good at sports.

"My father was an international rugby player," Paul says. "My mother was a very good athlete, as well, in softball [and] field hockey. [She] was [also] a dancer. So [the Kariya children] definitely have good genetics, which help. And I think we've all worked very hard at whatever we were doing, whether it was hockey or school."

Paul went to college at the University of Maine. It was far from home — on the other side of North America — but he loved the wooded campus. He also learned about hockey from Coach Shawn Walsh and continued to call on him for advice after leaving school.

It was at Maine where many hockey fans got their first look at Paul's rocket speed and blazing shot. His first season there (1992-93) was magical. The team nearly went unbeaten in the regular season, going 35-1-2 and averaging nearly six goals per game. Then it won the national championship in a thriller over Lake Superior State. Trailing 4–2 in the third period, Paul set up three goals by Jim Montgomery as Maine rallied for a 5–4 victory.

Paul had 100 points that season (25 goals plus 75

assists) and won the Hobey Baker Award as the best player in college hockey. It was enough to get him selected by the Mighty Ducks with the fourth overall pick of the 1993 NHL draft.

Chasing Olympic Glory
★★★★★★★★★★★

The NHL had to wait. Paul returned to Maine for his sophomore season. He then played for Team Canada in the 1994 Winter Olympics, in Lillehammer, Norway. Team Canada advanced to the gold-medal game, where it tied Sweden. Unlike the NHL, a shoot-out is used to break ties in Olympic competition. A shoot-out consists of five breakaways per team — shooter against goaltender — in a one-on-one battle. Paul scored one of the shoot-out goals, but when Peter Forsberg put Sweden ahead, Paul got another chance. This time, goalie Tommy Salo stopped him, and Sweden won the gold medal.

It was a disappointing finish, but Paul knew he was ready for the NHL. He's small by hockey standards — 5' 10", 173 pounds — but he quickly became one of the best players in the league. Through 1999-2000, Paul has had two 100-point seasons and one 99-point season. He has won the NHL's Lady Byng Trophy for sportsmanship two times, played in the NHL All-Star Game four times, and been named the league's best left wing three times. He also serves as captain of the Mighty Ducks.

What makes him so good? Look first at his skating.

STARS

RISING

STAT CITY
PAUL KARIYA

★**Team:** Mighty Ducks of Anaheim   ★**Position:** Left Wing

★**Acquired:** Drafted fourth overall in 1993

★**Born:** October 16, 1974, in Vancouver, British Columbia, Canada

★**Height:** 5-foot-10   ★**Weight:** 173 pounds

★**College:** University of Maine

★**Career Bests:** Is Mighty Ducks' all-time scoring leader with 464 points (210 goals, 254 assists) in 376 games.

★**Honors:** First Team All-Star in 1996, 1997, and 1999

★**Personal:** Single; hobbies include tennis, golf, swimming, weightlifting, and reading

---

"Everyone in our family kind of skates the same way," Paul says. "We have a very short, explosive stride. . . . We've got really good foot speed."

But it's more than that. Paul sees the ice very well and figures out where the puck is going to go. He's a student of the game. He's always watching from the bench and imagining things. No detail is too small for him.

Paul also benefits from hard work. He trains hard in the summer to build up his strength. He often stays late after practice to work on his game. Early in his career, he was unhappy with his backhand. (A left-handed shooter like Paul sweeps the puck from the *right* side to execute a backhand.) Paul spent countless hours trying to improve. Now he has one of the quickest and hardest backhands in the league.

The Odd Couple
★★★★★★★★★★★

P aul's NHL career really took off in February 1996, when the Mighty Ducks acquired high-powered winger Teemu Selanne from the Winnipeg Jets. (The Jets are now known as the Phoenix Coyotes.) Born in Finland, Teemu scored a record 76 goals for the Jets as a rookie, in 1992-93. He was just as fast as Paul.

"I would think the scariest sight for any defenseman would be Paul and Teemu attacking on a 2-on-1 break," said Ron Wilson, who was coaching the Mighty Ducks when Teemu joined the team.

The trade was great for Paul, who is quiet and soft-spoken. He had met the cheerful, bubbly Teemu at the 1996 All-Star Game and found him to be hilarious. Their personalities were so different that Jack Ferreira, the Mighty Ducks' general manager at the time, called them the odd couple.

"I'm a private person, very serious and focused on what I do," Paul says. "Teemu is the complete opposite. He's very easygoing and outgoing."

RISING

Teemu likes to crack jokes. He's also one of the friendliest superstars in the game. He enjoys signing autographs and is generous with his time. Paul is a little different. He's much quieter and takes the game seriously — almost too seriously at times. That's why the Selanne-Kariya partnership has helped both players.

"The way Paul analyzes the game is good for Teemu," says Coach Wilson, who is now coaching the Washington Capitals. "Teemu's ability to relax and have a little bit of fun has lightened Paul up enough so that he can enjoy a laugh every once in a while. Before, you never saw [Paul] smile. Now he's a lively guy in the dressing room."

Paul's career was zipping along when the NHL made an exciting announcement. The league would send its best players to the 1998 Winter Olympics, in Nagano, Japan. To get the Japanese people in the mood, the league also announced that the Mighty Ducks and the Vancouver Canucks would open the 1997-98 season with two games in Tokyo.

Because Paul's father was Japanese, the Japanese people were very excited. They considered Paul a hero. Unfortunately, Paul never made it to Japan. He missed the two games in October because of a contract dispute. He never played in the Olympics, either.

A Mighty Setback
★★★★★★★★★★★

On February 1, 1998, Paul was playing a game against the Chicago Blackhawks. He was near the Chicago net when defenseman Gary Suter of the Blackhawks hit him in the head with his stick. Paul was knocked to the ice. He became woozy. He was told he had a concussion, which is an injury to the brain.

Paul needed time to recover. He missed the Olympics and was sidelined for the remainder of the season. Team Canada could have used him in Nagano. They were the heavy favorites in the tournament, but came home without a medal.

That was nothing compared to what Paul was going through. He was suffering from headaches and memory loss. A concussion is a scary injury. Severe and repeated blows to the head have forced many players into early retirement.

"There were times when I thought about doing something else and not being able to play hockey," Paul says. "But even in times like that, I tried just to say, 'Forget

Paul's Hall of Fame Double

One of Paul's greatest attributes is the ability to anticipate plays before they develop. He's a great thinker and one of the most creative playmakers in the game. Combine that with his Gretzky-like vision and it's easy to see why so many people compare him to "The Great One." Wayne retired after the 1998-99 season as the league's all-time leading scorer. Like Paul, he helped make hockey a cool sport in Southern California.

about it. Don't worry about it right now. Just get better, and when you are better and feeling good, you can make a decision then.' Next thing I knew, everything had cleared and I was raring to go again."

Paul began feeling better in May 1998 and was cleared to play three months later. Wearing a better-padded helmet and a mouth guard, he returned for the 1998-99 season. Paul had 101 points and experienced no further concussion problems. Everyone was relieved.

Little Brother Joins the Party
★★★★★★★★★★★

Things are going well for Paul. His brother, Steve, went to Maine, won a championship, and was signed by the Vancouver Canucks. The Kariyas even played against each other for the first time in the NHL on December 8, 1999, at the Arrowhead Pond, in Anaheim, California. Paul scored a goal, and Steve had an assist as their teams played to a 2–2 tie. Their younger brother, Martin, might also play in the NHL someday. Like Paul and Steve, he, too, decided to attend Maine.

The Kariya boys are close, but they will always be competitive. Paul had never been able to beat Steve in checkers. But he solved it in typical Kariya fashion: hard work, dedication, and being a student of the game.

"I read a couple checkers books for some of our competitions, and I've beaten him handily," Paul says.

Why should we be surprised?

CHRIS DRURY

This gritty goal-scorer knows how to win a championship

★★★★★★★★★★★★

Center Chris Drury of the Colorado Avalanche is an excellent puckhandler and one of the fastest players on his team. He is also probably the only player in the NHL who talks more about baseball than he talks about hockey.

That's because so many people remember his outstanding performance at the 1989 Little League World Series, in Williamsport, Pennsylvania. Playing for Trumbull, Connecticut, Chris was chosen to pitch in the championship game, against Taiwan. He was only 12 at the time. The right-hander was a little chunky, standing 5' 1½" and weighing 126 pounds. Chris used his 66-mile-per-hour fastball to become a national hero. He pitched a complete-game five-hitter and knocked in two runs to give Trumbull a 5–2 win over Taiwan. It was a huge victory because Taiwan had won the Little League World Series 13 times since 1969.

15

Chris isn't the biggest guy around, but few players compete harder.

It was the first time that a team from the United States had won the Little League World Series since 1983.

"People seem to remember it vividly," Chris says. "They're not so interested that [I] play for the Avs."

Choosing Hockey
★★★★★★★★★★★★

Chris was born on August 20, 1976, in Trumbull. He has two older brothers, Ted and Jim, and a younger sister named Katie. The Drurys loved sports, but parents, Marcia and John, stressed academics and hard work.

Chris continued to play baseball throughout his teenage years. He competed in a Babe Ruth League and later made the varsity at Fairfield Prep High School, in Connecticut. "I did pretty well," he says. But at the same time, Chris was excelling at another sport — hockey. He was a whiz on skates and became a pretty good scorer at the high-school level.

That got Chris noticed by NHL scouts. In June 1994, he was drafted 72nd overall by the Quebec Nordiques. (A year later, the Nordiques moved to Denver, Colorado, where they were renamed the Colorado Avalanche.) Believe it or not, it was Chris's baseball experience that impressed many of the hockey scouts.

"I don't think any player in this draft has faced the kind of pressure he did when he was 12," Nordique scout Lewis Mongelluzzo told *USA Today* at the time. "[Baseball] was

America's pastime, and a worldwide television audience was watching him."

Although Chris lists former New York Yankee Don Mattingly as one of his heroes, he had to choose between baseball and hockey. He chose hockey and says the decision was pretty easy. Chris didn't see much of a future in baseball. He didn't think he would ever be good enough to reach the major leagues. He had also injured his wrist as a junior.

"There really wasn't much of a chance to do anything with [baseball]," Chris says. "Hockey always gave me a good opportunity to go to college for free, [to] get an education."

Big Man on Campus
★★★★★★★★★★★

Chris decided to put pro hockey on hold. He enrolled at Boston University in the fall of 1994. He quickly impressed his coaches with his willingness to work hard and lead his teammates.

"As a coach, it's impossible not to fall in love with the guy," says BU coach Jack Parker. "You say to yourself, 'This is exactly what we want everyone else to do.' The amount of intensity he showed in practice and the amount of focus we had in games were always determined by him."

Chris lit up the scoreboard. As a freshman, he helped BU win the NCAA Championship. In his sophomore year, he led Hockey East (the conference BU played in) with 42 points. (In hockey, goals plus assists equal points.) The following season, Chris led the conference in goals (27) *and* points (41). The thought of leaving college and jumping to the NHL crossed his mind.

"After my junior year, there was a real good possibility," Chris recalls. "I was thinking about it, talking about it with my family and my coaches. But, you know, it just didn't feel right. My gut feeling was to go back for my senior year. I felt I signed and accepted a four-year scholarship

STAT CITY
CHRIS DRURY

★**Team:** Colorado Avalanche   ★**Position:** Center

★**Acquired:** Drafted 72nd overall in 1994

★**Born:** August 20, 1976, in Trumbull, Connecticut

★**Height:** 5-foot-10   ★**Weight:** 185 pounds

★**College:** Boston University

★**Career Bests:** Scored 20 goals as a rookie in 1998-99 and matched that total the following season

★**Honors:** Won Calder Trophy as NHL's Rookie of the Year in 1998-99

★**Personal:** Single; older brother Ted has played center in the NHL since 1993.

STARS

at BU, and I wanted to honor that commitment."

Again, it was the right choice. Chris finished his BU career as the Terriers' all-time leader in goals with 113. As a senior, he won the 1998 Hobey Baker Award as the best player in college hockey.

For some reason, winners of that award seemed to struggle in the NHL. It's called the Hobey Baker jinx. Only wingers Neal Broten, who won the award with the University of Minnesota in 1981, and Paul Kariya, who won it with the University of Maine in 1993, had gone on to NHL stardom.

But Coach Parker was convinced that Chris would have a bright future in the NHL.

"What made me believe that he could play at the next level was his determination, and he got a lot faster," Coach Parker recalls. "He added strength from the waist down to become a better skater. Once he picked up that extra foot speed, everything else exploded for him."

Going Pro
★★★★★★★★★★

In 1998, Chris signed a pro contract and joined an Avalanche team loaded with talent. It had All-Stars like goalie Patrick Roy, centers Joe Sakic and Peter Forsberg, and defenseman Sandis Ozolinsh. Colorado had won the Stanley Cup in 1996, so Chris wasn't sure what kind of an impact he would make on the team.

"I didn't really know what to expect," Chris said, when

interviewed that season. "I didn't know what they had planned for me. I knew a lot of it was going to depend on how I adjusted. I'd say the biggest adjustment [was the] lifestyle change, moving to a new city. Obviously, it's a big difference [from] college. There's no homework. You're not surrounded by your friends and family. You're kind of off on your own, starting a new thing."

Chris was determined to make the Avalanche. At times he was in awe of his superstar teammates. He said he was overwhelmed the first day of training camp. Chris realized he was sitting in the same room with players he had watched on TV.

"After the first day, I realized they're just normal guys like you and me," he recalls. "They tie their skates the same way, tape their stick the same way. They're just great guys who are exceptional hockey players."

Rookie of the Year
★★★★★★★★★★★★

Chris made the Avalanche, along with winger Milan Hejduk [MEE-lon HEY-dook]. Milan, who is from the Czech Republic, had also been drafted by Quebec in 1994. Chris and Milan quickly made an impression with the Avalanche. Though Chris was small by NHL standards, at 5' 10" and 185 pounds, he played like someone who was a lot bigger. He used his speed to drive to the net. And he wasn't afraid to check bigger players.

Chris received plenty of help from his older teammates.

RISING

Chris's Hall of Fame Double

Chris battles hard to score his goals, just like former right wing Joe Mullen. Joe scored 502 of them in an NHL career that spanned 16 seasons from 1981-82 to 1996-97. He grew up in New York City and played at Boston College before entering the league with the St. Louis Blues. Joe played for the Blues, Calgary Flames, Pittsburgh Penguins, and Boston Bruins. He won Stanley Cups in Calgary (1989) and Pittsburgh (1991 and 1992).

He also learned from his brother, Ted, an NHL player and two-time United States Olympian. Ted, who is five years older than Chris, had played at Harvard University, in Cambridge, Massachusetts, before reaching the NHL with the Calgary Flames in 1993.

From watching his brother, Chris learned some of the things that are important to NHL players, such as how to eat the right foods, stay in shape, and get the proper rest away from the rink. Ted offered advice, but Chris basically learned by following his brother's example.

It must have been a good example. Chris finished the 1998-99 season with 20 goals and 24 assists in 79 games. That was good enough to earn him the Calder Trophy as the NHL's Rookie of the Year. Milan had 48 points (14 goals, 34 assists) and finished third in the voting. Marian Hossa, a gifted winger from the Ottawa Senators, was second.

"From the start of the year, [Chris and Milan] just kept getting better and better," said Avalanche captain Joe Sakic in 1999. "I think it was just huge that we got both of them this year."

Clutch Scorer
★★★★★★★★★★★

Chris continued his fine play during the 1999 playoffs. He scored six goals in 19 games as the Avalanche made it to the Western Conference finals before losing to the Dallas Stars. With four game-winning goals in the playoffs, Chris tied a rookie record set by winger Claude Lemieux of the Montreal Canadiens in 1986.

"It seems he has extra eyes for rebounds," says Avs Coach Bob Hartley. "He has a great hockey sense. You don't go to the net and find loose rebounds on your stick by luck."

Chris found plenty of loose pucks in 1999-2000. With more ice time, he scored the same number of goals (20), but improved his assist total from 24 to 47. In the playoffs, he added 4 goals and 10 assists for 14 points. That included a key goal in Game 6 of the Western Conference finals, against Dallas. With Colorado on the verge of elimination, Chris scored with 3:51 remaining to even the series.

Though Dallas won Game 7 to eliminate the Avalanche for the second year in a row, the future looks very bright for Chris. Maybe now, people will start asking him about hockey instead of baseball.

CHRIS DRURY

CHRIS PRONGER

This workhorse developed into the NHL's top defenseman

★★★★★★★★★★★

Defenseman Chris Pronger of the St. Louis Blues was named the NHL's Most Valuable Player and its best defenseman after the 1999-2000 season. He's one of the city's most popular athletes and is cheered almost everywhere he goes in St. Louis. So it's hard to believe that there was a time when the Blues' fans booed Chris so loudly and so much that he wanted to crawl into a hole in the ice.

The booing started shortly after Chris joined the Blues for the 1995-96 season. The fans in St. Louis were upset because popular All-Star forward Brendan Shanahan had been traded to the Hartford Whalers for Chris — so they took it out on Chris!

"I didn't realize the type of respect and the type of player Brendan had become in St. Louis," says Chris. "I knew he scored 50 goals in a season [twice], but I didn't realize what a pillar of the community he was and the

Opponents have a hard time standing up to Chris's strength and power.

RISING

things that he did off the ice that everybody loved him for."

Chris heard from the fans whenever he took the ice. Every time he made a mistake they let him have it even more. Chris didn't help himself by being lazy. He didn't work hard in practice and was often out of shape. It got to the point where he couldn't stand being jeered anymore.

Chris also got a helpful kick in the butt from his coach, Mike Keenan. Coach Keenan was called "Iron Mike" because of his no-nonsense ways. He *demanded* that his players work hard all the time. When Chris played horribly in a February 3, 1996, game against the Philadelphia Flyers, Coach Keenan benched him.

"I was miserable, and it was just one big mess," says Chris. "Then one day I just said, 'Forget it. Just play the game.' I was thinking negatively out on the ice."

Chris began putting more effort into workouts and practices. He was inspired by a new teammate — the great Wayne Gretzky — who had been traded to the Blues on February 27, 1996. Chris saw how Wayne made the most of his talents in every game.

"It was just a matter of trusting my instincts and going with the flow," Chris says. "Then things really started to move in the right direction for me. I gained a lot of confidence, and everything just kind of grew from there."

Chris went on to become a player worthy of loud cheers. In 1999-2000, he became just the second player in NHL history to win the Hart (MVP) and Norris (best defenseman)

Trophies in the same season. Bobby Orr of the Boston Bruins won both in the 1969-70, 1970-71, and 1971-72 seasons.

"The way [Chris has] developed over the last couple years is amazing," says Blues defenseman Al MacInnis. "I don't know if there's a player who's developed as quickly as he has."

De-Fense, De-Fense
★★★★★★★★★★★★

Christopher Robert Pronger was born on October 10, 1974, in Dryden, Ontario, Canada. He looked up to Bobby Orr, but became a defenseman because they got much more ice time than the forwards. Even then, Chris liked to play a lot of minutes!

Chris progressed through the ranks until he reached the Ontario Hockey League, in 1991. He played so well for the Peterborough Petes that NHL scouts started calling him "a young Larry Robinson." Larry was a great defenseman in the 1970's and 1980's. He won the Stanley Cup six times with the Montreal Canadiens. He coached the New Jersey Devils to the 1999-2000 Stanley Cup championship.

At 18, Chris was skinny as a rail. He stood 6' 6" but weighed just 180 pounds. The Hartford Whalers (now called the Carolina Hurricanes) took him with the second pick of the 1993 NHL draft. Although he was named to the league's All-Rookie team in 1993-94, he didn't become a star with the Whalers.

The team wanted Chris to gain weight so that he would

be stronger and not wear down during the long, punishing season. He tried to, but he couldn't keep the pounds on. Also, the team was struggling, and Chris wasn't playing as well as he could. He started to feel the pressure.

So when St. Louis traded for him on July 27, 1995, Chris welcomed the move, even though his first season turned out to be such a rocky one.

"You just need a change of scenery sometimes to wake you up," says Chris, "and I think Mike Keenan really helped me when I first got here. I guess you [would] call it tough love. He was pretty hard on me, but it forced me to look in the mirror and try to fix the flaws in my game. It took probably the first full year I was here to really come into my own and start playing the way I knew how to. Nothing comes easy."

Asserting Himself
★★★★★★★★★★

Chris improved steadily and was named captain of the Blues on September 29, 1997. Then his game *really* took off. He became a dominant physical force. And he was almost impossible to get around. At age 23, Chris was a finalist for the Norris Trophy and led the league with a plus-47 rating in 1997-98. (In hockey, when each team has the same number of skaters on the ice, a player receives a "plus" when his team scores a goal. He gets a "minus" when the opposing team scores.)

Chris helped the Blues sweep the Los Angeles Kings in

the first round of the 1998 playoffs. In the next round, against the Detroit Red Wings, he continued his dominance. In Game 5 of that series, on May 17, Chris played nearly 29 minutes and helped kill off nine St. Louis penalties. Detroit eventually won the series, but Chris was awesome.

Well-Conditioned Athlete
★★★★★★★★★★★

What makes Chris so good? First, his conditioning is fabulous. Being in top shape allows Chris to play a lot of minutes at a high level. An average defenseman plays 20 to 25 minutes in a 60-minute game. Chris averaged a league-leading 30 minutes 14 seconds per game in 1999-2000. And he says he doesn't even get tired!

"I feel pretty good after a game," he says. "Some games — depending on the amount of skating, the type of game — I feel a little worn down, and other games I feel real fresh. If we are killing a lot of penalties, then I'll be a lot more tired. . . . But for the most part, I feel pretty good."

Secondly, Chris's body has matured. He no longer struggles to maintain his weight. He weighs 220 pounds — 40 pounds more than when he was drafted — and much of it is muscle.

In 1997, Chris began working with a trainer named Charles Poloquin, in Colorado Springs, Colorado. Chris visits him during the early part of the off-season to receive a specialized fitness program. He finds out how

RISING

much to run, how much to lift, and which foods to eat. Chris works out six days a week during the summer and returns to Colorado periodically for fitness testing.

Double Threat
★★★★★★★★★★★

Chris was a good scorer in junior hockey, but he wasn't much of a threat offensively at the start of his NHL career. He had only 37 goals over his first five seasons. But things changed before the 1998-99 season when right wing Brett Hull and defenseman Steve Duchesne left the Blues as free agents. Their departure left a huge hole on the power play. Chris was given the opportunity to fill it. (In hockey, teams go on the power play — or a man advantage — when the other team takes a penalty. It's easier to score in such situations.) In 1998-99, Chris had 13 goals, and eight were scored on the power play.

"He's a great passer, and he's got a great shot from the blue line," says Al. "He's a threat to score. He sees the ice well. When you lose two guys like Duchesne and Hull and still maintain a pretty good power play, it's a credit to the players that have filled in, like Pronger."

The best defensemen contribute on offense *and* defense. That gets you noticed, and Chris was opening eyes around the league. He was selected to play for Team Canada at the 1998 Olympics, in Nagano, Japan. In 1999 he played in his first NHL All-Star Game. And at the 2000 All-Star Game, fans voted him to start for the North American team.

Some players would be satisfied with those accomplishments. But Chris realizes he can do a lot more. "You are always in a constant struggle for perfection," he says. To that end, Chris has become a better leader. He tries to stay away from dumb penalties, something he didn't do earlier in his career.

A Season to Remember
★★★★★★★★★★★★

Everything came together for Chris and the Blues in 1999-2000. He stepped up his game even more. He set career highs in goals (14), assists (48), and points (62). He led the league again with a plus-52 rating. And under his leadership, the Blues had the NHL's best record (51-20-11). Unfortunately, the San Jose Sharks upset the Blues in the first round of the playoffs, four games to three.

That playoff loss was disappointing, but there was

Chris's Hall of Fame Double

With his long reach, physical presence, and improving offensive skills, Chris reminds people of Larry Robinson. Larry coached the New Jersey Devils to the 1999-2000 Stanley Cup title. But before that, he played 20 seasons in the NHL, from 1972 to 1992, and his teams never missed the playoffs. Larry won six Stanley Cups with the Montreal Canadiens, a feat that Chris would surely love to emulate.

RISING

still awards night in Toronto, Ontario, Canada, on June 15, 2000. Chris took home the Norris and the Hart, two of the most important trophies. The voting for the Hart (MVP) was the closest in NHL history. Chris edged winger Jaromir Jagr of the Pittsburgh Penguins by just one vote.

"Who do I have to thank?" joked Chris, as he looked out at a sea of reporters.

The answer was simple: himself.

STAT CITY
CHRIS PRONGER

★**Team:** St. Louis Blues   ★**Position:** Defenseman

★**Acquired:** Traded from the Hartford Whalers to the St. Louis Blues on July 27, 1995, in exchange for left wing Brendan Shanahan

★**Born:** October 10, 1974, in Dryden, Ontario, Canada

★**Height:** 6-foot-6   ★**Weight:** 220 pounds

★**Career Bests:** Led NHL with plus-47 rating in 1997-98 and plus-52 rating in 1999-2000

★**Honors:** Won Hart (MVP) and Norris (best defenseman) Trophies in 1999-2000

★**Personal:** Engaged; enjoys golfing, fishing, and boating

OLAF KOLZIG

A longtime backup becomes "The Man" in Washington

★★★★★★★★★★★

Goaltender Olaf Kolzig of the Washington Capitals is an intimidating target. He is 6' 3" tall and weighs 226 pounds. The net is just four feet high and six feet wide, so Olaf can cover most of it — even when he's standing still. And when opponents get close, they come face to face with Godzilla!

A picture of the famous fire-breathing movie monster is painted on top of Olaf's mask. The nickname *Zilla* is printed on the bottom, right across his chin. Olaf was playing for a minor-league team in Rochester, New York, during the 1992-93 season. He was dubbed "Godzilla" by some fans because of his size and fiery temper. Since becoming the Capitals' star netminder in 1997, Godzilla has been a menace to any shooter who dares to challenge him. He loomed large during the 1999-2000 season, winning the Vezina Trophy as the NHL's best goaltender.

Kick save and a beauty! Few players are able to beat "Olie the Goalie."

Olaf is bigger than most netminders, but he's extremely quick. He has good reflexes and an excellent glove hand. He likes to challenge the shooter and will even leave his crease to chase down loose pucks.

World Traveler
★★★★★★★★★★★

Olaf was born on April 6, 1970, in Johannesburg, South Africa. His parents are from Germany. They were working in the hotel business in Johannesburg when Olaf was born. (Because of his mother and father, Olaf is a German citizen. This allows him to play for Germany in international events, such as the Olympics.)

The Kolzigs moved to Copenhagen, Denmark, when Olaf was 2. A year later, they moved to Edmonton, Alberta, Canada. That's where Olaf began playing hockey. The family then lived in five other Canadian cities before settling in Union Bay, British Columbia. Olaf got used to packing his bags. He did it again in 1988 when he moved to Kennewick, Washington, to play for the Tri-City Americans of the Western Hockey League.

Olaf did well in the Western League, going 16-10-2, with a 3.48 goals-against average (GAA), during the 1988-89 season. The Capitals were impressed. They liked his athleticism and selected him in the first round of the 1989 NHL draft. In the second round, they chose Byron Dafoe, another goalie from the Western League. Byron later achieved NHL success with the Boston Bruins.

RISING

"We went to Russia in our first [training] camp with the Capitals," says Byron. "There, we became really good friends. It was very competitive."

Olaf made the Capitals after a strong training camp in 1989. It was quite an accomplishment because he was only 19 years old. Most goalies don't reach the NHL until they are in their twenties. Olaf played two games for Washington at the start of the 1989-90 season, but gave up 12 goals and was sent back to Tri-City.

Temper, Temper
★★★★★★★★★★★

It took Olaf a long time before he was ready to return to the NHL for good. That's not unusual. Goalies usually take longer to develop than forwards or defensemen. Goaltender is a demanding position, and young ones have a lot to learn. Even the best goalies, such as Patrick Roy of the Colorado Avalanche and Martin Brodeur of the New Jersey Devils, have spent at least some time in the minor leagues.

After his junior career in Tri-City, Olaf worked on his game in the East Coast Hockey League and the American Hockey League. He had good size and quick reflexes, but his temper was a problem. If he gave up a goal, he got very angry and lost his concentration. That made it easier for the other team to score again, which would only make Olaf madder. "He used to snap a lot," says Byron.

Goalies hate to be scored upon — even in practice! Olaf had to learn how to let go of his anger and concentrate on the next shot. It wasn't easy but Olaf got better at it as he grew older. Call it maturity.

In 1993-94, Olaf and his pal Byron helped the Portland (Maine) Pirates win the American Hockey League championship. Olaf was named MVP of the playoffs, and the two goalies shared an award for allowing the fewest goals during the regular season. That should have been Olaf's ticket to the NHL. He made the Capitals in the fall of 1994, but the league was shut down by a labor dispute. That kept Olaf on the sideline for four months, until the owners and players resolved their differences.

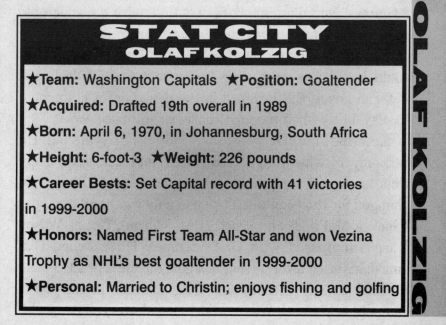

STAT CITY
OLAF KOLZIG

★**Team:** Washington Capitals ★**Position:** Goaltender

★**Acquired:** Drafted 19th overall in 1989

★**Born:** April 6, 1970, in Johannesburg, South Africa

★**Height:** 6-foot-3 ★**Weight:** 226 pounds

★**Career Bests:** Set Capital record with 41 victories in 1999-2000

★**Honors:** Named First Team All-Star and won Vezina Trophy as NHL's best goaltender in 1999-2000

★**Personal:** Married to Christin; enjoys fishing and golfing

OLAF KOLZIG

Career Backup?
★★★★★★★★★★★

Olaf spent most of 1994-95 and 1995-96 with the Capitals as a backup to Jim Carey. Jim struggled in the first round of the 1996 playoffs, against the Pittsburgh Penguins, and Olaf got the call. Washington lost the series, but Olaf won a lot of admirers with his stingy 1.94 GAA. He did his best work in Game 4, which lasted an amazing four overtimes! He made a club-record 62 saves before giving up the game-winning goal to Pittsburgh center Petr Nedved.

Olaf was the backup again in 1996-97. He played in only 29 games, compiling a record of 8-15-4, with a respectable 2.59 GAA. Jim Carey continued to struggle, so he was traded to the Boston Bruins on March 1 of that season. It could have been Olaf's big break, but the Capitals got veteran goalie Bill Ranford in the deal. Olaf was burning to play, but he had to learn another skill: patience.

Entering the 1997-98 season, Olaf was 27 years old. He had only 14 wins in his NHL career, and it seemed likely that he would remain a backup goalie. But things had changed for the Capitals. They had a new general manager (George McPhee) and coach (Ron Wilson). Coach Wilson wasn't impressed with Olaf's temper. He watched Olaf smash his stick after letting in a goal during a practice, and decided to say something. "That doesn't show you're competitive," Coach Wilson said. "That shows you're a jerk."

Olaf listened to his coach and tried to keep his anger in check. He began the season as Bill Ranford's backup. Then came the big break that Olaf had been waiting for.

One Man's Pain is Another Man's Gain
★★★★★★★★★★★★

On October 1, 1997, the Capitals opened the season against the Maple Leafs in Toronto, Ontario, Canada. Bill Ranford started, but didn't last long. He was hit by a shot and had to leave the game with a groin injury. Olaf got off the bench and began to stretch. He was a little nervous. But then he reminded himself: "Here's your opportunity. Just give the guys a chance to win."

That's just what he did. The Capitals won, 4–1, and won six of their next seven games.

"I started to believe in myself," Olaf recalls. He kept playing, and the Capitals kept winning. The goalie who seemed destined to become a career backup was playing so well that *Bill Ranford* was riding the bench. Olaf was selected to play in his first NHL All-Star Game. He also went 2–0 for Germany at the Winter Olympics, in Nagano, Japan. By the end of the NHL regular season, Olaf had won 33 games. He was ready for the playoffs.

Olaf's old pal, Byron Dafoe, had enjoyed a great season with the Bruins. The Capitals met the Bruins in the first round. Olaf and Byron put their friendship on hold. Olaf and the Caps won the series, four games to two. In Round 2, the Capitals beat the Ottawa Senators in five

RISING

games. Olaf clinched the series with back-to-back shutouts. Then Washington knocked off the Buffalo Sabres, four games to two, to advance to the Stanley Cup finals.

Olaf was on fire. He and the Caps needed only four more wins to capture the Stanley Cup, the ultimate dream of any hockey player. But it wasn't to be. The favored Detroit Red Wings beat the Capitals in four straight games to win the Cup.

Bouncing Back
★★★★★★★★★★★

Washington rewarded Olaf with a new contract, but the team failed miserably in 1998-99. The Capitals were rocked by injuries and missed the playoffs. When 1999-2000 began, things changed for the better. The Capitals began winning in December and didn't stop. In January, Olaf went 11-1-2, with a 1.68 GAA. He was named the NHL's Player of the Month. He soon became the talk of the league.

Olaf was chosen to play in the 2000 NHL All-Star Game. When the season resumed, Washington sailed into first place in the Southeast Division. Olaf was the league's hottest goalie. He made 52 saves in a 2–2 tie with the Detroit Red Wings on March 3. It was clear that he was operating with a laser-like focus.

"I think the players have a lot of respect for him as a person," says George McPhee, the Capitals' general manager. "Outside of just being a heck of an athlete, he's a quality guy, a mature person, well-adjusted and likeable."

Olaf finished the regular season 41-20-11, with five shutouts and a 2.24 GAA. It seemed as if Washington was good enough to return to the finals. But it didn't happen. The Capitals faced their old nemesis, the Penguins, in the first round of the playoffs. The Penguins eliminated them in five games.

That stinging loss didn't matter when it came time for the NHL to hand out its annual awards. Most NHL trophies are presented for a player's performance during the regular season. Olaf was the hands-down winner of his first Vezina Trophy. It was clear that a new goaltending monster was on the loose.

Olaf's Hall of Fame Double

Like Olaf, Ken Dryden was a big goaltender who liked to challenge the shooter. Standing 6' 3" tall and weighing 210 pounds, Ken enjoyed a relatively brief career with the Montreal Canadiens (eight seasons), but what a run he had! Ken played on six Stanley Cup winners and compiled a record of 258-57-74 in 397 NHL games. He left hockey in 1979, at the age of 31, and is now the president of the Toronto Maple Leafs.

Vincent's skill and maturity helped him become the youngest captain in NHL history.

VINCENT LECAVALIER

This youngster can strike quickly — like lightning!
★★★★★★★★★★★★

Center Vincent Lecavalier *[luh-KAV-uhl-YAY]* of the Tampa Bay Lightning has always been described with glowing words.

When he played junior hockey, in the Canadian province of Quebec, scouts were awed by his smooth moves and flashy goal-scoring and called him a "pure talent." When he was taken with the first pick of the 1998 NHL draft, the owner of the Lightning predicted that Vincent would become "the Michael Jordan of the NHL."

Okay, that was going a bit too far. But one thing is clear: Vinny, as he is called by his teammates, is blessed with special skills on the ice.

"There's really nothing he doesn't have," says Lightning general manager Rick Dudley. "He's got size [6' 4", 205 pounds]; he's got speed; he's got magical hands; he's got grit."

He's also very mature for his age. That's why the Lightning named him, at 19, the youngest captain in NHL history, on March 11, 2000.

Vinny had filled in as captain earlier in the 1999-2000 season after center Chris Gratton was sidelined with an injury. Then Chris was traded to the Buffalo Sabres.

"I would guess that seven to ten of our players said to me that they liked Vinny as a captain," Mr. Dudley recalls. "That's significant. Virtually everyone was older than [Vinny]. It tells you something about the kid."

Born to Play
★★★★★★★★★★

Vinny was born on April 21, 1980, in Ile Bizard, Quebec, near Montreal. He seemed destined for a big future. He began skating at the age of 2, which, he says, is a year earlier than most kids start in hockey-crazed Quebec. He began playing organized hockey at 4.

Vinny says he was always a good offensive player. But his great work ethic made him stand out.

"[My father, Yvon] always told me the most important thing was to work hard," Vinny recalls. "Sometimes, you can have three goals, but you're not working. If you don't have a point, but you work hard and do your best, that was the right thing to do."

When he was 14, Vinny left home to enroll at the Notre Dame school in the province of Saskatchewan. The school's hockey program has produced NHL players such as forward Rod Brind'Amour (Carolina Hurricanes) and goalie Curtis Joseph (Toronto Maple Leafs). In his second season at Notre Dame, Vinny scored 104 points in just 22 games.

Vinny thought the best way to be a high draft pick in the NHL was to return home and play against the tougher competition in the Quebec Major Junior Hockey League. Many gifted scorers, including number one picks Mario Lemieux (formerly of the Pittsburgh Penguins) and Pierre Turgeon of the St. Louis Blues, had played there.

It was a good decision. In 1996-97, Vinny was named the top rookie in Canadian junior hockey after netting 42 goals and 61 assists in 64 games with the Rimouski Oceanic. The following season, he had 44 goals and 71 assists in just 58 games.

Realizing a Dream
★★★★★★★★★★★★

The last-place Lightning paid close attention to Vinny's exploits. They had made the playoffs only once since entering the NHL, in 1992. They needed a big star, so they made Vinny the top draft pick in 1998.

"I was really happy," says Vinny. "It's everyone's dream to be first overall or a first-round pick. Since I was seven or eight years old, I watched the draft every year, hoping that one day it could be me."

Number one picks often feel pressure. So when Lightning owner Art Williams said Vinny was going to be the Michael Jordan of hockey, many people cringed.

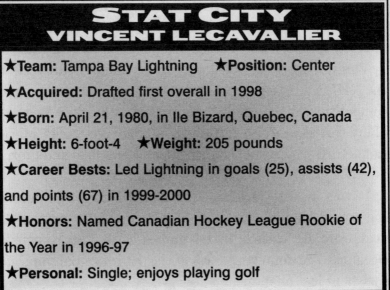

STAT CITY
VINCENT LECAVALIER

★**Team:** Tampa Bay Lightning   ★**Position:** Center

★**Acquired:** Drafted first overall in 1998

★**Born:** April 21, 1980, in Ile Bizard, Quebec, Canada

★**Height:** 6-foot-4   ★**Weight:** 205 pounds

★**Career Bests:** Led Lightning in goals (25), assists (42), and points (67) in 1999-2000

★**Honors:** Named Canadian Hockey League Rookie of the Year in 1996-97

★**Personal:** Single; enjoys playing golf

They feared it would turn up the heat on Vinny to an unbearable level. But Vinny kept his cool.

"He came in with a real low-key attitude, not a 'I'm the first pick overall, here I am to save the franchise' type of attitude," says Jacques Demers *[de-MAIR]*, who coached Vinny during his rookie season in the NHL. "He was very respectful of coaches. He fit in with the players. He was an 18-year-old kid, and in my mind, he was thinking like he was 21 or 22 or even older."

Coach Demers had 13 years of NHL coaching experience and knew how to handle young stars. He had coached forwards Doug Gilmour in St. Louis and Steve Yzerman —

Vinny's idol — in Detroit when both were young. Coach Demers believed in letting young players develop slowly.

"The Lightning had been known to burn a lot of the young kids in the past, and we weren't going to do that [with Vinny]," Coach Demers recalls.

Coach Demers let Vinny play only eight to nine minutes per game at first, which isn't much. Star forwards usually play 20 or more minutes per game. Vinny wanted to play more, but he never complained. "My first year was a year where I had to learn and watch what the veterans did on the ice," he says.

Coach Demers loved Vinny's attitude.

"This is a kid who was brought up the way Gretzky's father brought up Wayne — with respect," says Mr. Demers. "He doesn't make statements that he's going to look back on and regret. [Vinny's] father was a strict disciplinarian, and he taught him the right way."

New League, New Challenge
★★★★★★★★★★★

It was good that Vinny was given the chance to learn slowly. He found the NHL tough going at first.

"Players are stronger in the NHL and everybody's good," he says. "The intensity level is higher. It took me about fifteen to twenty games, then it was going a lot better after that."

After 50 games, Vinny got more playing time and more chances to score. In February 1999, he was named the

RISING

NHL's Rookie of the Month after getting four goals and three assists in 11 games.

Vinny finished the season with 13 goals and 15 assists in 82 games. He knew he needed to get stronger during the summer in order to win battles with the NHL's big defensemen. So he put on 15 pounds — all of it muscle.

The Lightning, who finished last again, made changes. They had a new owner, who brought in a new general manager and coach for the 1999-2000 season.

Steve Ludzik, the new coach of the Lightning, liked Vinny's skill. He put Vinny on the power play and told him to "have fun" with the puck. By February 2000, Vinny was having a blast. He had equaled his rookie-season point total of 28, and had dominated at times, scoring 4 points in one game and 3 points in two others.

"In your second year, you feel more comfortable," Vinny says. "In my first year, I was nervous every game. I think confidence is a big part. When you have the puck and you're not nervous with it, that's the key."

Becoming a Star
★★★★★★★★★★

Vinny is at his dazzling best when he races down the ice and sets up a teammate. So Mr. Dudley, the new general manager, tried to find the right linemates for him to work with. Winger Mike Johnson was acquired from the Toronto Maple Leafs on February 9, 2000. The line of Vinny, Mike, and winger Todd Warriner clicked right away. Vinny responded with 29 points in his final 28 games.

"Vinny emerged as a player when [Coach Ludzik] put those three together," Mr. Dudley says. "They're smart; they can skate; they have good size; and they're blessed with offensive abilities. When Vinny starts doing his thing, someone has to [know] where they need to go to be open, and Mike seems to be able to do that very well."

Vinny became the Lightning's best player. That made him the right choice as captain. He was thrilled, and did his best to lead by example.

"It's not just his offense," Mr. Dudley says. "Vinny wants to be a great defensive player, too. He plays tough. He doesn't mind sticking up for a teammate. He'll fight if he feels it's in the interest of the team. When you're sitting on the bench and you [see how he plays], you say, 'Well, I guess I can play that way, too.' "

Vincent's Hall of Fame Double

Vincent is an elegant skater who wears number 4 and hails from the province of Quebec. That also describes the classy Jean Beliveau, who played 20 seasons with the Montreal Canadiens, from 1950 to 1971. Jean was a tall center who recorded 507 goals and 1,219 points in 1,125 games. He also played on 10 Stanley Cup winners. That's one Stanley Cup ring for each finger!

VINCENT LECAVALIER

RISING

Bright Future
★★★★★★★★★★★

Vinny led the Lightning in goals (25), assists (42), and points (67) in 1999-2000. He is expected to become a 100-point scorer within the next few seasons. Scoring 100 or more points in a season is a special accomplishment that isn't easy, even for the NHL's brightest stars. But Vinny doesn't like to talk about things like that. He always puts the team first.

"The biggest thing is for the Lightning to get better," Vinny says. "Personally, I want the same thing. I want to get better every game."

Vinny's two goals should go hand in hand. The Lightning are a young team and should improve as their youngsters mature and improve with experience. Vinny will be a big part of that.

"This is a no-miss," says Jacques Demers. "I think this kid is destined for a great future because of his mental approach to the game. Just like the great players I've coached, he loves practicing and he loves playing the game. I think he's going to be extremely, extremely successful."

With glowing words like those to describe him, maybe Vinny should wear shades on the ice!

PATRIK ELIAS

Watch out! This guy is a game-breaker
★★★★★★★★★★★

Last-second, game-winning goals are rare in hockey. Basketball great Michael Jordan was famous for his buzzer-beating shots. Game-winning home runs in the bottom of the ninth inning are fairly common in baseball, as are game-winning touchdowns and field goals as the clock expires in a football game. But in hockey, a game-winning goal with a second or two left is as rare as seeing snow on July 4.

That's why it was so exciting when left wing Patrik Elias *[EL-ee-osh]* of the New Jersey Devils performed such a feat on January 26, 2000.

Patrik had been the hottest player in the NHL for over a month leading up to that game. He and the Devils were playing against the Florida Panthers at the National Car Rental Center in Sunrise, Florida. With the game tied at 2–2, the teams were just seconds away from overtime. Robert Svehla *[SVAY-la]*, a defenseman with the Panthers,

Head up and in control, Patrik leads the charge up ice.

had the puck deep in his team's zone. Instead of letting time expire, Robert tried to pass. Bad move! Patrik intercepted the puck. He skated right at goalie Mike Vernon and calmly flipped in the winning goal with 1.7 seconds left in the third period. Patrik stunned the Florida crowd into silence. His teammates exploded in joy.

"It was a great feeling," Patrik said after the game. "Just shows it's not over till it's over."

Making His Mark
★★★★★★★★★★★★

Patrik brings an exciting style of play to the usually colorless Devils. They are plodding and cautious. He is fast and creative. For a long stretch during the 1999-2000 season, he strutted his flashy stuff in almost every game.

Unsigned at the start of training camp, Patrik missed the first nine games of the regular season. He finally agreed to a contract with the Devils, but it took him awhile to get going. Once he did, he started to score goals in bunches! Patrik popped in 20 goals during a 21-game stretch in December and January. He also set a Devil record by notching at least 1 point in 15 consecutive games. He played in the NHL All-Star Game and finished the season with 35 goals and 37 assists for 72 points. His goal and point totals led the Devils.

"He's a person who, in my mind, at least, is someone who wants to be the best at what he does," Devil General

Manager Lou Lamoriello told the Bergen County (New Jersey) *Record.* "He doesn't compete against other players; he competes against himself.

"That's something we've seen in him all along. He wants to get the most out of himself, and to me, that's a tremendous quality to have."

And one that makes for rare, and exciting goals.

Czech This Out
★★★★★★★★★★

Patrik was born in Trebic, Czech Republic, on April 13, 1976. Like many Europeans, he grew up playing soccer as well as hockey. At 15, Patrik left his hometown to enroll at a hockey academy in the city of Kladno. In European countries, promising athletes are often invited to such academies, or schools. Patrik met Petr Sykora at the academy, and both played on the Czech junior national team. The two would later become teammates — and best friends — on the Devils.

The Devils made Patrik a second-round draft choice in 1994, but he stayed in his homeland for the 1994-95 season, posting four goals and three assists in 28 games with Kladno.

The next year, at age 19, Patrik left for the United States. Like most prospects, he had to prove himself in the minor leagues before reaching the NHL. That meant a trip to Albany, New York, the home of the Devils' top farm team, the Albany River Rats. Patrik found success there in 1995-96, recording 27 goals and 63 points in 74 games.

Patrik spent most of 1996-97 in Albany, netting 67 points in 57 games. Even then, he was displaying the skills that would make him a star in the NHL. Patrik is a good passer and playmaker. He is a swift skater and can blast a shot while at full stride. He's not afraid to charge the net, and even the biggest, nastiest, most physical opponents don't intimidate him.

Patrik was named to the NHL's All-Rookie team in 1997-98 after posting 18 goals and 19 assists in 74 games with the Devils. The following season, he scored 17 goals in the same number of games, but nearly doubled his assist total to 33. That set the stage for 1999-2000, when

STAT CITY
PATRIK ELIAS

★**Team:** New Jersey Devils ★**Position:** Left Wing

★**Acquired:** Drafted 51st overall in 1994

★**Born:** April 13, 1976, in Trebic, Czech Republic

★**Height:** 6-foot-1 ★**Weight:** 200 pounds

★**Career Bests:** Led Devils in goals (35), points (72), and power-play goals (9) in 1999-2000

★**Honors:** Named to NHL's All-Rookie team in 1997-98

★**Personal:** Single; enjoys soccer and music

RISING

he and his linemates — center Jason Arnott and right wing Petr Sykora — were very possibly the best forward line in the league.

Unstoppable Force
★★★★★★★★★★★

The Arnott-Elias-Sykora line was put together by former Devil coach Robbie Ftorek in February 1999. When Coach Ftorek was fired and Larry Robinson replaced him in March 2000, Coach Robinson thought he would break up the trio. In hockey, it's not always good to have your three best scorers on the same line. The other team will focus on stopping that line, and if the other team succeeds, there's a good chance your team will have trouble scoring. Some coaches believe it will cause more headaches for the opposition when top scorers are used on two, or even three, lines.

Coach Robinson's decision to separate Patrik and his linemates lasted one game. That was all it took for Coach Robinson to realize that the Arnott-Elias-Sykora line worked so much better than any other lines he could put together. So the terrific trio was reunited. No line, on any team, played better in the 2000 Stanley Cup playoffs. Patrik had seven goals and 13 assists; Jason had eight goals and 12 assists, and Petr potted nine goals with eight assists.

The Devils' magic line rescued the team after it fell behind the Philadelphia Flyers, three games to one, in the Eastern Conference finals. In the do-or-die Game 5,

Patrik, Jason, and Petr each put the biscuit in the basket to trigger a clutch 4–1 win. The Devils won Game 6, 2–1, before Patrik broke the Flyers' hearts in Game 7 by scoring both goals in a 2–1 win that sent the Devils into the Stanley Cup finals, against the Dallas Stars.

The Stars were the defending Cup champions. The Devils, though, had enough weapons to shoot down the Stars. Leading three games to two, the Devils traveled to Dallas, Texas, for Game 6. The game was a brutal defensive struggle that went into double overtime, tied at 1–1. Then Patrik made a heroic play. With the puck in the Dallas end of the ice, he fired a no-look pass to the side of the net where Jason was waiting. Jason knocked it past Star goalie Ed Belfour, and just like that, the game was over. The Devils won the Stanley Cup!

Thinking of a Friend
★★★★★★★★★★★

While the big, gleaming silver Cup was being presented to the Devils, there was an emotional moment. Patrik had Petr's jersey (which is called a "sweater" in hockey) wrapped around his shoulders. Earlier in the game, Petr had been knocked to the ice by a booming check from Star defenseman Derian Hatcher. Petr was carried off the ice on a stretcher and taken to the hospital with a concussion.

Patrik felt bad that his best friend and teammate wasn't there to share in the celebration. So he draped Petr's

RISING

sweater over his back because he knew Petr was watching the game on TV at the hospital. Coach Robinson, who won six Stanley Cups as a defenseman with the Montreal Canadiens, walked over to Patrik, took the sweater, and slipped it on himself.

"I wanted to wear it in honor of Petr," Coach Robinson said after the game. "But I felt Patrik also deserved to have everybody see the name on his *own* sweater."

Mr. Popularity
★★★★★★★★★★★

Patrik is well-liked by his teammates. He loves to make jokes, and often cracks up his teammates with the way he says things in English.

"He's just a funny guy," Jason says. "He loves re-phrasing lines from movies. He's always saying something from one of those Austin Powers movies or *Dumb and Dumber*. You know, *those* kind of movies. His kind of movies.

"There are just some days when you come in here all tired and down and out, and he does something to put a smile on your face. That's what I like about him. You just like to have someone like that around."

Patrik has adjusted well to the United States. He lives in a New Jersey condominium during the season and spends much of his free time in New York City, just minutes away. Patrik enjoys movies, trendy restaurants, and going to the theater.

"On the ice, off the ice, I'm very happy with myself," he says. "Of course, I like this lifestyle. Who wouldn't? This is a fun game to play, and right now, I'm just having a great time."

Teammate Bobby Holik adds: "I think Patty is a genuinely good kid."

And a genuinely good hockey player.

Patrik's Hall of Fame Double

Patrik's first coach in the NHL was Jacques Lemaire, who had been a terrific playmaking center during his career with the Montreal Canadiens. Jacques won eight Stanley Cups as a player and later coached the Devils to their first Cup title, in 1995. He had 366 goals and 835 points in 853 regular-season games and averaged nearly a point per game during the playoffs. Like Patrik, Jacques was a terrific passer who inspired his linemates.

JOE THORNTON

He's no ordinary Joe! This guy is ready to dominate

★★★★★★★★★★★

Joe Thornton of the Boston Bruins is used to being the *center* of attention.

For starters, Joe is hard to miss. The bruising Bruin center is 6' 4" and 220 pounds. He has been nicknamed Big Bird because of his height and wavy blond hair.

Joe was the first player chosen in the 1997 NHL draft. He has an amazing ability to see and analyze the action on the ice and make nifty passes that lead to goals. He works hard along the boards, isn't afraid to drive to the front of the other team's net, and shoots the daylight out of the puck.

Joe became a big name in Boston during his first three NHL seasons. When reporters from newspapers in other cities showed up at practice, Bruin coach Pat Burns knew there were only two players the reporters would ask him about.

Joe is developing into a great player, although not as quickly as some people would like.

"Okay, is it Ray Bourque or Joe Thornton?" Coach Burns would ask.

Defenseman Ray Bourque is a future Hall of Famer. (He played for the Bruins for 21 seasons before being traded to the Colorado Avalanche in March 2000.) Now, Coach Burns spends his time talking about Joe.

Joe completed his third NHL season in 1999-2000 by leading the Bruins in goals (23), assists (37), points (60), and penalty minutes (82). When a player racks up a lot of penalty minutes, it means he is playing with a great deal of physical intensity. For Joe, that intensity was born in the backyard of his childhood home in Canada.

Childhood Battles
★★★★★★★★★★

Joseph Eric Thornton was born in London, Ontario, Canada, on July 2, 1979. He grew up in St. Thomas, Ontario (pop. 40,000), with his parents, Mary and Wayne, and two older brothers, Alex and John. Joe began playing hockey at the age of 4, after his dad flooded the backyard to create a "rink."

"I would play with other neighborhood kids and my brothers," Joe says.

Joe and his brothers played pickup games every chance they could. The games were rough, but Alex and John claim that Joe (the smallest of the three) initiated a lot of the physical play. At one point, their mom told them they couldn't play anymore because too many games were ending in fistfights.

When Joe was 16, in 1995, he moved away from home to play for the Sault Ste. *[SOO saint]* Marie Greyhounds of the Ontario Hockey League. The Greyhounds have produced many NHL players over the years. Want some examples? How about "The Great One," Wayne Gretzky, the all-time leading scorer in NHL history? Or All-Star center Ron Francis (Carolina Hurricanes)? How about goalie John Vanbiesbrouck (New York Islanders)?

It didn't take long for Joe to have his own effect on the Greyhounds. In 1995-96, he was named the top rookie in Canadian junior hockey, after bagging 30 goals and 76 points in 66 games. The following season, he produced a mind-blowing 122 points (41 goals, 81 assists) in only 59 games to finish second in the Ontario League scoring race.

Joe also represented Canada at the 1997 World Junior Championships. The WJC is an Olympic-style tournament for the best teenage hockey players in the world. At 17, Joe was the youngest player on his team. That didn't matter, though, as he posted two goals and two assists in seven games to help Canada win a gold medal.

Another Lindros?
★★★★★★★★★★★

NHL scouts were predicting a great future for Joe. As a 17-year-old, he was the most-talked-about prospect since Eric Lindros, in 1991. Joe was often compared to Eric, the Philadelphia Flyer superstar.

RISING

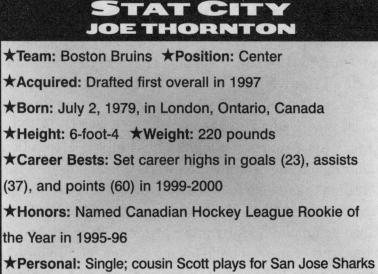

STAT CITY
JOE THORNTON

★**Team:** Boston Bruins ★**Position:** Center

★**Acquired:** Drafted first overall in 1997

★**Born:** July 2, 1979, in London, Ontario, Canada

★**Height:** 6-foot-4 ★**Weight:** 220 pounds

★**Career Bests:** Set career highs in goals (23), assists (37), and points (60) in 1999-2000

★**Honors:** Named Canadian Hockey League Rookie of the Year in 1995-96

★**Personal:** Single; cousin Scott plays for San Jose Sharks

Joe was almost as big as Eric, played the same position, and had a good scoring touch like Eric.

The Bruins had a horrible season in 1996-97, finishing with a record of 26-47-9. There's only one good thing about finishing so poorly. You get a high pick in the next draft! With the first pick in the 1997 draft, the Bruins chose Joe.

Draft day was one of the greatest moments of Joe's life, but he had a hard road ahead of him. It's very difficult for an 18-year-old to skate right in and make an impact in the NHL. Teenagers don't have the experience to compete against grown men. The Bruins thought about sending Joe back for another season of junior hockey. But how much more could he accomplish in Sault Ste. Marie? The Bruins decided to keep Joe in Boston instead. And Joe quickly learned that scoring goals would not be as easy in the NHL as it was in junior hockey.

"It was hard for me at first," Joe says. "I thought I was going to be a star right away because that's what I was used to. But then I struggled. I didn't play defense good enough because I never had to as a junior. It wasn't easy. Suddenly, you're always under a microscope."

Rough Beginning
★★★★★★★★★★★

Joe had only three goals and four assists in 55 games during his rookie season. Fans and management were frustrated. Some people had expected Joe to become the next Cam Neely. Cam was one of the most popular Bruins when he played for Boston from 1986-96. He was a rugged winger who produced three 50-goal seasons for the Bruins.

"Someone asked me, 'When is Thornton going to be Cam Neely?' " Coach Burns told *Sports Illustrated* in 1998. "I said, 'Oh, how about 2005? He'll be 26. He'll be in his prime. He'll be a [heck] of a player. That's how long it takes some guys.' "

Cam wasn't an overnight sensation, either. He was just 18 when he entered the NHL with the Vancouver Canucks in 1983. Cam scored 51 goals over his first three seasons, but that wasn't enough for the Canucks.

Joe's Hall of Fame Double

Joe is built like the great Bruin center Phil Esposito. One of the strongest players of his time, Phil was virtually unmovable once he parked himself in front of the net. He recorded 717 goals and 1,590 points in 18 NHL seasons with the Chicago Blackhawks, Bruins, and New York Rangers. Phil was the first player to score 100 points in a season (1968-69). He also held the NHL record for goals in a season (76 in 1970-71) until Wayne Gretzky broke the mark with 92 in 1981-82.

They traded him to the Bruins, in 1986, and he soon developed into one of the best power forwards of his era.

Finding His Way
★★★★★★★★★★★

Joe made great progress in 1998-99, his second NHL season. Appearing in 81 games, he improved his goal total from 3 to 16. He also boosted his point total from 7 to 41. But it wasn't enough to silence some of his critics. They complained that he lacked intensity at times. They also said he needed to improve his defensive skills.

Some players would be hurt by such comments. Joe wasn't. He kept his chin up and kept working hard. He sparkled during the 1999 playoffs, posting three goals and six assists in 11 games. That gave Joe extra confidence for the 1999-2000 season. He drilled home 23 goals and 37 assists in 81 games. Those were good numbers, but *still* not good enough for some folks in Boston.

Harry Sinden, the Bruin general manager, told Joe that he has a long way to go. "He's one of the best prospects in the game, but right now he's only that," Mr. Sinden told the Worcester (Mass.) *Telegram*. "His development, in my opinion, is not where it should be. It's not bad, but it's not where it should be."

Joe's response? "I keep getting better each year, so that's all I'm worried about."

Becoming "The Man"
★★★★★★★★★★★

When Joe wasn't scoring, Coach Burns put him on the Bruins' checking line. That line's job was to focus on defense by smothering the other team's top line with tight checking. On February 7, 1999, Joe was assigned to play against Wayne Gretzky of the New York Rangers. Joe did his job to perfection! He held "The Great One" scoreless and actually delivered the game-winning goal himself to lift the Bruins to a 3–2 win. "Whenever you go against Gretzky, it's a fun time," Joe said afterward. "I've never played against him so it was extra special for me. To get the game-winner was special also."

Joe was starry-eyed when he first got to the NHL. After three years in the league, he is still awed by some of the stars he plays with and against. "Pavel Bure is

RISING

unbelievable," Joe says of the Florida Panther superstar. "He scores goals by the bundles."

Joe has started to adjust to NHL life. He's getting his own apartment after living with a Boston-area family during his first three seasons. Joe had lived with Tom and Nicole Hynes, and their children, Vanessa and Todd. The Hynes family had taken in young Bruins in the past. They treated Joe like one of their own, and Mrs. Hynes even helped Joe answer his fan mail.

The mail should continue to flow because Joe has plenty of fans. One group of guys sits high in the balcony of the FleetCenter, Boston's home arena. Each one of them has a letter of Go Joe painted on his T-shirt. Before games, they go down to ice level to cheer for Joe and the Bruins as they warm up.

"You can always hear them screaming during games," Joe says, "even though they are way up at the top of the building. I'm not sure what the fans beside them are thinking, because if I can hear them on the ice, I can just imagine how loud they must be up there."

Perhaps those fans are wondering why Joe has yet to lead the NHL in scoring. All they have to do is be patient. Joe's enormous talent is still blossoming. It won't be long before the spotlight, and the full attention of the hockey world, will be focused on Big Joe, the scoring king.

JEFF FRIESEN

You don't want to mess with this Shark

★★★★★★★★★★★

Being picked on is never pleasant, and it is not limited to kids at school or on the playground. Adults get picked on, too. Would you believe that it happened to one of the best players on the San Jose Sharks after he joined the team?

When left wing Jeff Friesen *[FREEZ-in]* was an 18-year old rookie, in 1994, some of his older teammates gave him a very hard time. They mocked him and made rude comments at times. To his credit, Jeff rose above it and became one of the league's most feared scorers.

Shark Coach Darryl Sutter thinks Jeff is a stronger and better player today *because* of the things that happened to him. Through his first six NHL seasons, from 1994-95 through 1999-2000, Jeff recorded 137 goals and 177 assists for 314 points. He's San Jose's all-time leader in each of the three categories.

Nicknamed "Freeze," Jeff can score in a variety of ways.

Rude Welcome
★★★★★★★★★★★

When Jeff first entered the Sharks' dressing room, he sometimes felt as if it was him against the world. The Sharks had failed to win with older players, so the team's management was bringing in younger ones like Jeff. Several of the veterans were upset. The veterans felt threatened by the youngsters, who were trying to replace them, and they didn't like the idea of losing their highly paid jobs. This created a split between the older and younger players on the team.

Jeff had wanted to develop a good relationship with the veterans. Their knowledge and experience can make them excellent teachers, and some veterans do enjoy taking rookies under their wings and helping them. Rookies are often asked by veterans to perform good-natured tasks. Jeff had no problem with that. He would willingly unpack the veterans' equipment bags and even start their cars in the airport parking lot after arriving from a road trip.

Jeff was also deeply respectful of the team's head coach, Kevin Constantine. Coach Constantine appreciated this, but it didn't sit well with Jeff's older teammates.

"Some veterans were envious of all these kids making big money right away," recalls defenseman Jeff Norton, an older player on the Sharks who actually befriended his young teammate Jeff. "Mostly, they were envious of Friesen's talents. He was a great kid, a great player, but some guys at the time were cruel. They called him teacher's pet and Kevin's son.

"Anything extra [Jeff] did in practice wasn't viewed as a kid trying to make himself better, but as kissing up," Jeff Norton adds. "I spent a lot of time that year telling him, 'Don't worry, you're going to be around a lot longer than those guys.'"

Natural Scorer
★★★★★★★★★★

Jeff was born on August 5, 1976, in Meadow Lake, Saskatchewan, Canada. His favorite player growing up was Steve Yzerman, the longtime captain of the Detroit Red Wings. Steve can score goals, but he also excels at the defensive aspects of the game. Jeff wanted to be a great all-around player like Steve.

Jeff was a hotshot in youth leagues. He progressed rapidly and eventually landed with the Regina Pats of the Western Hockey League. Jeff scored 45 goals for the Pats in 1992-93 and 51 the following season.

It looked as if Jeff would be the first player chosen in the 1994 NHL entry draft. But in the months leading up to the draft, there were whispers that Jeff was lazy and that all he cared about was scoring goals. The rumors were false, but the damage was done. Jeff fell out of the top 10. San Jose grabbed him with the 11th overall pick.

"He's probably the most caring young player I've seen," says Shark general manager Dean Lombardi.

"[Jeff] fell to eleventh in the draft because the knock was that he was soft, that he didn't care, that all he was concerned about was his points. He's been the complete [opposite]. He'll get two goals and afterward be [critical of himself]. He's never satisfied, almost to a fault."

Jeff needed that determination to survive his tough rookie season. One day in practice, Jeff replaced a veteran on one of the Sharks' top lines. Every time Jeff shot the puck, the vet would mimic him. It went beyond the point of good-natured teasing. And Jeff wasn't the only youngster who got picked on. Defenseman Mike Rathje grew so

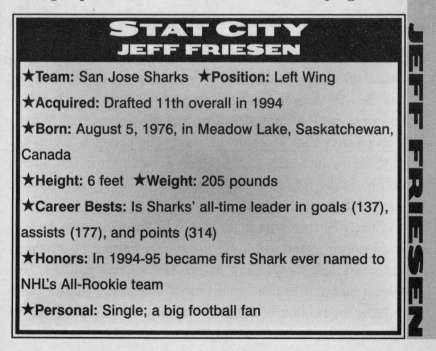

STAT CITY
JEFF FRIESEN

★**Team:** San Jose Sharks ★**Position:** Left Wing

★**Acquired:** Drafted 11th overall in 1994

★**Born:** August 5, 1976, in Meadow Lake, Saskatchewan, Canada

★**Height:** 6 feet ★**Weight:** 205 pounds

★**Career Bests:** Is Sharks' all-time leader in goals (137), assists (177), and points (314)

★**Honors:** In 1994-95 became first Shark ever named to NHL's All-Rookie team

★**Personal:** Single; a big football fan

frustrated about the abuse he was taking from older players that he started to pin them against the wall in practice.

"I never did that, although there were times I felt like doing it," Jeff told *Sports Illustrated* in 1999. "You take it and take it, and there comes a point where you've had it."

The razzing from his teammates didn't seem to affect Jeff's play. The 1994-95 season was shortened to 48 games because of a labor dispute between the owners and the players. Jeff finished with 15 goals and 10 assists for 25 points. He became the first Shark ever named to the NHL's All-Rookie team.

Changing His Style
★★★★★★★★★★★

Jeff believes he made his greatest strides as a player after the Sharks hired Coach Darryl Sutter before the 1997-98 season. Coach Sutter wasn't happy with Jeff's flashy style. He wanted Jeff to "get his nose dirty." When a coach says that, it means he wants the player to compete with more intensity and become a battler for the puck. Jeff had been a finesse player, relying on pretty moves and a good shot to score most of his goals.

Coach Sutter was a former NHL player who had a hard-nosed reputation. He was determined to change Jeff, and Jeff was willing listen. He became grittier. He began to park himself in front of the other team's net, looking for rebounds and deflections to tip past the goalie. Many players aren't willing to do that because of the sticks, elbows, and punishing checks they take from opposing defensemen. But Jeff wasn't afraid. In his first season under Coach Sutter, Jeff posted career highs in goals (31) and points (63).

"It was a big eye-opener to me when Coach Sutter came," Jeff says. "I finally [felt like I was] learning and improving."

Coach Sutter admits he pushed Jeff hard when the coach came to San Jose.

"Freeze and I had to get to know each other, especially early in [1997]," Coach Sutter says. "I felt I had to push him. Now it's more reinforcement."

Positive Influences
★★★★★★★★★★★

Jeff also credits forwards Bernie Nicholls and Tony Granato with helping him mature as a player. The two veterans came to San Jose during the 1996-97 season. Bernie, who has since retired, and Tony were supportive, not like the other veterans Jeff had to deal with at the start of his career.

"Bernie was a guy who really helped me as soon as he got here," Jeff says. "When I'd come off the ice [after a bad shift] saying 'I'm awful,' Bernie and Tony would tell me 'Hey, kid, shut up! You're a good player, and quit saying you're not!' All of a sudden, I'd think, 'Hey, if these guys think I'm good, maybe I am.'"

In 1997-98, two more positive influences arrived in San

RISING

Jose. Goalie Mike Vernon was acquired from the Detroit Red Wings. Mike had won two Stanley Cup titles and was the MVP of the 1996-97 playoffs. Winger Dave Lowry was acquired from the Florida Panthers. Dave was a respected veteran because he was a jokester who liked to have fun with the younger players.

"We now had all these guys who made you feel good about yourself, instead of laughing at you, trying to ruin your confidence, which is what happened my first two years," Jeff says.

Becoming a Leader
★★★★★★★★★★★★

Jeff gained even more confidence on October 28, 1998, when the Sharks named him an alternate captain. An alternate captain wears an *A* on the front of his jersey. The *A* means that Jeff is considered one of the leaders of his team. A captain has the right to discuss calls with the referee during the game. When the captain is not on the ice, an alternate captain (maximum of two per team) assumes that responsibility. Jeff enjoys his role of alternate captain. That's not surprising for someone who still looks up to one of the greatest captains in NHL history — Steve Yzerman of Detroit.

"Steve took a little bit away from his point totals to play better defense so that he could lead his team to a championship," Jeff says. "Hockey is such a team game. If you try to be a team player first, everything else should take care of itself."

Jeff saw Steve accomplish *his* goals by winning back-to-back Stanley Cups in 1997 and 1998. If Jeff continues to improve, he believes he can do likewise in San Jose.

The Sharks believe they are getting closer. After collecting 26 goals and 35 assists in 1999-2000, Jeff helped San Jose upset the St. Louis Blues in the first round of the 2000 playoffs. Jeff had two goals in the seven-game series, including one in the deciding contest. Unfortunately for him and the Sharks, they were eliminated by the Dallas Stars in the second round.

Jeff's career is thriving. The rough treatment he got from the veterans made him tougher because he was able to fight his way through it. Winning a Stanley Cup will be every bit as tough a challenge. But you can bet your milk money that Jeff will be up to it.

Jeff's Hall of Fame Double

Jeff is an excellent skater who can weave his way through traffic or score with opponents draped all over him. In that sense, he's like former Philadelphia Flyer Bill Barber. A left wing, Bill collected 420 goals and 883 points in 12 seasons with the Flyers from 1972 to 1984. He played on Stanley Cup winners in 1974 and 1975.

MILAN HEJDUK

Need a clutch goal? Just call on the Avs' young dynamo
★★★★★★★★★★★

It's always fun to watch a player's reaction in the first few seconds after he scores a goal. Most players raise their sticks in triumph. Others pump their fist the way golfer Tiger Woods does after sinking a long putt. On March 26, 2000, winger Milan Hejduk *[MEE-lon HEY-dook]* of the Colorado Avalanche celebrated a goal in a more zany way.

The Avs were playing their archrival, the Dallas Stars, at Reunion Arena, in Dallas, Texas. The game went into overtime as 17,001 fans and a national television audience waited to see who would break the 1–1 deadlock. The answer was Milan. He made a nifty move on defenseman Darryl Sydor and whipped the puck over goalie Ed Belfour with 1:43 left in overtime. Milan let out a whoop and skated to center ice. He then flopped on his stomach

Quick hands and a nose for the net have helped Milan become one of the NHL's top goal-scorers.

and began dog paddling, as if he were trying to stay afloat in a swimming pool.

"It was just a reaction," Milan told the *Denver Post*. "I'll probably only do that once."

Milan may only do the dog paddle on ice once, but he will be scoring plenty of goals for years to come.

Rocky Mountain Magic
★★★★★★★★★★★

Milan made quite a splash by starring on Colorado's "Kid Line," with center Chris Drury and rookie winger Alex Tanguay during the 1999-2000 season. Milan played fearlessly along the boards and in front of the net. Like many goal-scorers, it seemed as if the puck followed him around the ice. Milan led the Avs in goals (36) and game-winning scores (9) while finishing second in points (72) that season. He also played in all 82 regular-season games for the second year in a row. That was important because two of the Avs' best players, centers Peter Forsberg and Joe Sakic, missed long stretches of the season because of injuries.

"He reads the play really well," says former Colorado winger Dave Andreychuk. "He's in the right position all the time, and for a young guy, that's amazing. He always knows where the puck is going. It took me quite a few years to get to the level he's at right now."

Milan has soft, skillful hands that allow him to handle the puck like a wizard and score breathtaking goals with a variety of wicked shots. San Jose Shark coach Darryl Sutter compares Milan to former New York Islander Mike Bossy. A Hall of Famer, Mike scored 50-or-more goals nine times, finishing with a career total of 573.

"[Milan] is definitely a natural scorer, a future superstar," says teammate Peter Forsberg. "The goals he scores are unbelievable. He knows exactly where to go."

Sporting Family
★★★★★★★★★★★

Milan Hejduk, Junior was born on February 14, 1976, in Usti-nad Labem, Czech Republic.

STAT CITY
MILAN HEJDUK

★**Team:** Colorado Avalanche ★**Position:** Right Wing

★**Acquired:** Drafted 87th overall in 1994

★**Born:** February 14, 1976, in Usti-nad Labem, Czech Republic

★**Height:** 5-foot-11 ★**Weight:** 185 pounds

★**Career Best:** In 1998-99, led NHL rookies in points during the regular season (48) as well as the playoffs (12)

★**Honors:** Named to NHL's All-Rookie team in 1998-99

★**Personal:** Single; enjoys golf, tennis, and soccer

RISING

His dad, Milan Hejduk, Senior, coaches hockey in the Czech Republic. Mr. Hejduk directs a team in Teplice, a city of about 50,000 people located near the country's northern border with Germany. Mr. Hejduk and his wife, Blanka, have lived for years in the larger Usti-nad Labem (pop. 90,520), about 10 miles away.

"When I started to play hockey, I was five years old or so," Milan says. "I spent a lot of time in the rink. And right next to that, there were tennis courts and my mother was a tennis player. So I spent my time on tennis and hockey."

With parents who loved sports, it wasn't surprising that young Milan was athletic, but he was a bit of a late bloomer. He scored just six goals in 22 games for Pardubice of the Czech League in 1993-94, but scouts from the NHL's Quebec Nordiques liked his potential. Quebec drafted Milan 87th overall in June 1994. (The Nordiques moved to Denver, Colorado, the following year and became the Colorado Avalanche.) Milan wasn't ready for the NHL, so he remained with Pardubice for four more seasons and improved his numbers to 27 goals in 51 games, in 1996-97, and 26 goals in 48 games, in 1997-98.

Making the Move
★★★★★★★★★★★

A successful stint with the 1998 Czech Olympic team convinced Milan he was ready to come to North America. He helped the Czechs win the gold medal at the Winter Games, in Nagano, Japan. Led by acrobatic goalie Dominik Hasek and superstar forward Jaromir Jagr, the Czechs upset Canada and Russia to shock the world of hockey.

"The Olympics were the first time I got to play with [Milan]," Jaromir told the *Denver Post*. "He didn't get to play in our first two games, but he came out in that third game [with] absolutely no fear at all."

The Avs were certainly impressed. They signed Milan the following summer. Like many Europeans who come to North America to play in the NHL, Milan had problems learning English. He knew almost none when he reported to his first training camp, in 1998.

"I can be so much better in English," he says, "but I am getting better. I learned a lot from TV. I watched a lot of movies and I spent a lot of time with my teammates, and that helped me."

Milan also took English lessons from a private tutor. He even got some help from his roommate on the road, winger Adam Deadmarsh of the Avalanche. "He literally didn't know a word of English," Adam told Denver's *Rocky Mountain News*. "He would just stand there while the coaches were talking to us with this blank look on his face. You could tell he didn't understand a thing. But now he understands just about everything. It just goes to show you how smart the guy is. Learning a foreign language is tough."

RISING

Rookie Sensation
★★★★★★★★★★★

In 1998-99, Milan led NHL rookies with 48 points on 14 goals and 34 assists. He was also a finalist for the Calder Trophy, which is presented to the league's Rookie of the Year. Milan finished third in the voting behind his teammate, center Chris Drury, and winger Marian Hossa of the Ottawa Senators. Milan might have gotten more support from the hockey writers who vote for the award if he had scored more goals. Chris had 20 that season. Marian had 15. Milan had 14.

"[In 1998-99], I didn't score a lot of goals, but I got a lot of chances, a lot of shots," Milan recalls. "I am still learning about goalies. ... If you shoot low, you have a great chance to score in Europe. Not here. You have to shoot high."

That's because North American goalies play a different

Milan's Hall of Fame Double

San Jose Shark Coach Darryl Sutter says that Milan reminds him of former New York Islander winger Mike Bossy. Armed with great hands and a booming shot, Mike was one of the best goal-scorers in NHL history. "The Boss" scored 50-or-more in nine consecutive seasons and finished with 573. Mike was one of the kingpins of the Islander dynasty during the 1980's. He helped the team win four consecutive Stanley Cup titles from 1980-83.

style than the ones in Europe. North American goalies tend to go down more frequently. Therefore, you have to shoot the puck high to beat them. European netminders like to stay on their feet. To score on them, you need to keep the puck low.

Milan had a solid rookie season, but it ended early when he suffered a broken collarbone against the Stars in Game 4 of the 1999 Western Conference finals. The injury might have cost Colorado a chance to win the Stanley Cup. Milan had to watch as the Avs blew a three games-to-two lead in the series. The Stars came back to win in seven before defeating the Buffalo Sabres to win the Cup.

Who knows what would have happened if Milan, who had six goals in the 1999 playoffs, including two overtime winners, was in the lineup? Milan led NHL rookies with 12 points during the post-season. He also became the first rookie since 1939 to score two overtime winners in one playoff series. He did it in the first round against the San Jose Sharks.

"It was frustrating," Milan says. "I wish I could have played. But injuries are part of the game. There's nothing you can do. I was pretty sad I couldn't play in the important games, especially that Game 7. That was very hard to take."

Fitting In
★★★★★★★★★★★

n 1999-2000, Milan established himself as one of the most underrated young stars in the NHL. There's a good reason for that. A lot of people overshadow him in Colorado. Joe Sakic and Peter Forsberg are superstars. Patrick Roy is one of the greatest goaltenders in the history of the NHL. Defenseman Ray Bourque is a future Hall of Famer. The team itself challenges for the Stanley Cup year after year. But Milan fits right in.

"On top of being a great goal-scorer," Colorado Coach Bob Hartley says, "he's probably one of the smartest hockey players in the NHL in the [offensive, defensive, and neutral] zones. He reacts to every situation; he never panics, and I think he shows a lot of poise."

Adds Joe Sakic, "Whenever the game's on the line, he likes to have the puck. He really seems to like playing in overtime and in pressure situations."

"I have more confidence, and I feel more comfortable with the type of game here in the NHL," Milan says. "It takes some time to figure out what's going on here. It's totally different. You don't have much time [to react] because the rink is smaller and the other players are closer to you. You have to think quicker than in Europe."

Get used to hearing the name Milan Hejduk. Expect his spectacular plays and extraordinary goals. Maybe he will even celebrate one by doing the dog paddle again.

SCOTT GOMEZ

There's no mystery to this Alaskan's game

★★★★★★★★★★★

Who has the best smile in pro sports? Here's a vote for winger/center Scott Gomez of the New Jersey Devils. He seems to walk around 24 hours a day with a big grin plastered to his face. But, hey, if you were Scott, you would smile, too.

Scott had a rookie season to remember in 1999-2000. He made a huge jump from junior hockey — where he played for Tri-City of the Western Hockey League — to immediate success in the NHL. He led all first-year players in scoring with 70 points (19 goals, 51 assists) and played in the All-Star Game. He won the Calder Trophy as the NHL's Rookie of the Year. And, oh, yeah, he helped the Devils win the Stanley Cup!

Not bad.

Scott's big season included all kinds of amazing accomplishments and marvelous performances. Perhaps

Nicknamed "Gomer," Scott helped the Devils win the Stanley Cup in a memorable rookie season.

the most special of all was that Scott served as a pioneer for the Latino community: He became the first Hispanic to play in the NHL. "Definitely an awesome year," Scott says.

Indeed.

Native Alaskan
★★★★★★★★★★★

S cott was born in Anchorage, Alaska, on December 23, 1979. He is one of a handful of native Alaskans to make it to North American professional sports. One of the others is NBA guard Trajan Langdon of the Cleveland Cavaliers. Trajan graduated from Anchorage East High School, the same school that Scott attended.

Scott's father, Carlos, was one of 10 children born to a migrant Mexican farm worker in Modesto, California. Scott's mother, Dalia, was born in Medellin, Colombia. She was raised by an aunt in Brooklyn, New York.

Scott's dad was a hockey fan. When he lived in San Diego, California, Mr. Gomez rooted for a minor league team known as the San Diego Gulls. His favorite player was Willie O'Ree. On January 18, 1958, Willie became the first black to play in the NHL when he suited up for the Boston Bruins. He was hockey's version of Jackie Robinson, who broke baseball's color barrier in 1947.

Carlos moved from San Diego to Alaska in 1972. Some of his older brothers had moved there in the 1960's and '70s to work in construction. Carlos was an ironworker.

Dalia moved from Colombia to Brooklyn, in 1961, to live

with an aunt. They relocated to Alaska two years later. Carlos and Dalia met when she was in high school. She was 17. They married about a year later.

Being born in Alaska, Scott has certainly heard a lot of jokes about his state. He *did not* grow up living in an igloo. He *did not* dogsled to school or wear snowshoes, either. Anchorage is a modern city of 250,000 people, with lots of indoor ice rinks and shopping malls.

Natural Talent
★★★★★★★★★★★

Scott began playing organized hockey at the age of 5. He would go to college games at the University of Alaska–Anchorage. But a lot of his education came from playing against his mother.

"I used to play goalie, if you can call it that," Dalia Gomez told NHLPA.com, the official website of the NHL Players' Association. "When Scott first started getting into hockey, he would just keep going for hours. I would be exhausted, but he still wanted to play. Indoors or outdoors, it didn't matter. Scott would get me to strap pillows to my legs and my chest, and I'd play goalie.

"There were always a lot of kids in the house when Scott was growing up," adds Mrs. Gomez. "A lot of stuff ended up getting broken, but we didn't care. Our house took a beating on the inside. There were a lot of bumps and dents everywhere from all the hockey that was played indoors. But it never mattered to us. We had so many good times that the odd broken lamp or table was never a worry."

When Scott began skating, he had trouble staying on his feet. He told his mom that he wanted to quit hockey. She said, "Sure." But that didn't sit well with his dad.

"He fell on his butt a couple of times. He was a mama's boy, and he was whining," says Carlos Gomez. "I'd just spent $50 for a new pair of skates. No way am I going to let him quit the first day."

Scott, who was twice named Alaska's Player of the Year at Anchorage East High School, has certainly come a long way since then. Seeking stiffer competition, he moved to Surrey, British Columbia, Canada, in 1996, to play for a Canadian junior team. The following year, he moved again — to Kennewick, Washington — to join the Tri-City Americans of the Western Hockey League. He had 12 goals and 37 assists in 45 games for the Americans, in 1997-98. That caught the eye of the Devils, who chose him in the first round of the 1998 NHL draft.

The Devils are well known in the NHL for their ability to draft and develop young talent. Scott went back to Tri-City for the 1998-99 season. He showed great improvement, racking up 30 goals and 78 assists in 58 contests.

Unexpected Break
★★★★★★★★★★

Scott was not expected to contend for an NHL roster spot during the 1999-2000 season. The Devils like to give their young players a few seasons of

STARS

RISING

STAT CITY
SCOTT GOMEZ

★**Team:** New Jersey Devils ★**Position:** Center/Left Wing

★**Acquired:** Drafted 27th overall in 1998

★**Born:** December 23, 1979, in Anchorage, Alaska

★**Height:** 5-foot-11 ★**Weight:** 200 pounds

★**Career Bests:** Led NHL rookies in assists (51) and points (70) in 1999-2000

★**Honors:** Won Calder Trophy as NHL's Rookie of the Year in 1999-2000

★**Personal:** Single; Scott's personal trainer is Vladimir Bure, the father of Florida Panther star Pavel Bure

professional experience in the minors before they join the big club. But fate intervened on Scott's behalf. Two Devils — forwards Patrik Elias and Brendan Morrison — had contract disputes during training camp. Scott was given a chance to fill one of the empty roster spots, and he made the Devils with a strong showing in training camp. He became the first Hispanic to play in the NHL when he made his regular-season debut for New Jersey on October 2, 1999, against the Atlanta Thrashers.

Scott impressed everyone with his poise and smart decisions. A gifted playmaker, he quickly became one of the league's best passers. Although better known for his passing, Scott can also score. He recorded a hat trick on December 26, 1999 — three days after turning 20 — against the rival New York Rangers at Madison Square Garden, in New York City. Scott scored all three of New Jersey's goals in a 3–3 tie. It was even more special that his parents were there to see him do it.

Earning Praise
★★★★★★★★★★★

Devil captain Scott Stevens is amazed at how cool, calm, and collected Scott is at such a young age. The rookie would often relax in the dressing room lounge just minutes before a game.

"I thought it would just happen for a while, but he's just laid-back, easygoing," Scott says. "He has confidence. He doesn't get flustered. Twenty minutes before games he's lying on a couch reading the paper, la-di-da. He doesn't get nervous before games."

And what about his game on the ice?

"I'm real impressed," Scott Stevens adds. "He very rarely turns the puck over, and he draws players on the other team out of position. He knows before he gets the puck what he's going to do with it. Most guys have to collect it first and then look around and decide what to do with it."

Scott's vision and playmaking ability drew raves during his rookie season. He's quick, plays solid defense, and even has a nasty side. Any opponent who dishes out a solid check

SCOTT GOMEZ

on Scott can be sure to receive a harder one in return.

"He's almost like an old-school player in the now generation," Devil general manager Lou Lamoriello told the Los Angeles *Times*. "He has God-given ability to see plays prior to those plays developing. He makes other players better."

"Scott understands the game a lot," says Devil goalie Martin Brodeur. "He's one of those guys who you play with that you just know is going to be a star for many years to come."

The Pioneer
★★★★★★★★★★★

Scott capped his magical rookie season by helping the Devils win the Stanley Cup. He had four goals and six assists in 23 playoff games. And like all players who win the Cup, Scott was allowed to take it home for a day during the summer. It was the first time the Cup had ever been to Alaska!

There were autograph signings, parades, and police escorts. Anchorage thanked Scott for a year of memories and thrills. And Scott thanked them back for their support.

In front of thousands of fans, Scott hoisted up Lord Stanley's big silver Cup and exclaimed: "There it is! This is yours, too. Kiss it, grab it, do whatever."

It's a feeling that Scott says he can get used to. Many players go their entire careers without getting to experience such a moment. But Scott says he's not going to let success spoil him.

"I know I'm lucky," he says. "I know my job is playing a game, and I appreciate that and am thankful for that. This is my only career, so I plan on having fun and making the most of it. The first year was memorable, but I hope my entire career will be, too."

Scott is also aware of his special place in hockey history. "Being Latino and playing professional hockey is definitely something I am proud of," he says. "If my playing in this league inspires other Latinos to try this sport, if it gives other Hispanic kids a reason to believe they can make it to the NHL, then that's something that I'm thrilled about."

Just what Scott needs: *another* reason to smile!

Scott's Hall of Fame Double

With great vision and a knack for finding the open man, Scott is a crafty playmaker like former Chicago Blackhawk center Stan Mikita. Stan played 22 seasons, from 1958 to 1980, racking up 541 goals and 926 assists for 1,467 points. He led the league in scoring four times and twice won the Hart Trophy as the NHL's MVP. Stan was also the first big-name player to wear a helmet, even though it wasn't considered cool at the time.

WANT TO HAVE MORE FUN

WITH SPORTS ILLUSTRATED FOR KIDS?

GET A FREE TRIAL ISSUE of SPORTS ILLUSTRATED FOR KIDS magazine. Each monthly issue is jam-packed with awesome athletes, super-sized photos, cool sports facts, comics, games, and jokes!

Ask your mom or dad to call and order your free trial issue today! The phone number is 1-800-732-5080.

PLUG IN TO www.sikids.com. That's the S.I. FOR KIDS website on the Internet. You'll find great games, free fantasy leagues, sports news, trivia quizzes, and more.

CHECK OUT S.I. FOR KIDS Weekly in the comic section of many newspapers. It has lots of cool photos, stories, and puzzles from the Number 1 sports magazine for kids!

LOOK FOR more S.I. FOR KIDS books. They make reading *fun!*